ITALIAN PRIMITIVES

*Panel Painting of the Twelfth
and Thirteenth Centuries*

ITALIAN PRIMITIVES

Panel Painting of the Twelfth
and Thirteenth Centuries

Text by

ENZO CARLI

HARRY N. ABRAMS, INC., *Publishers* NEW YORK

Library of Congress Catalog Card Number: 65-18186

Copyright in Italy by SILVANA EDITORIALE D'ARTE, Milan

Printed and bound in Italy

CONTENTS

LIST OF ILLUSTRATIONS

Black-and-White Illustrations

COLORPLATES

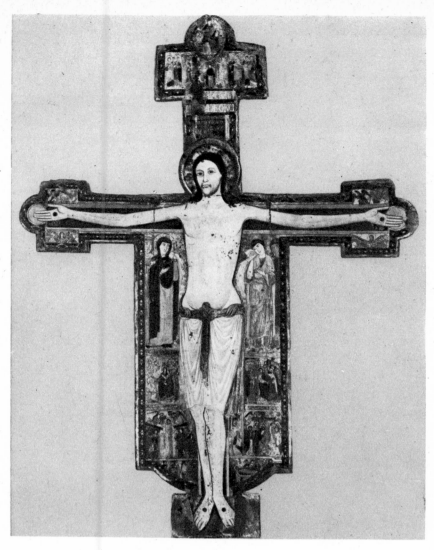

Fig. 1 - GUGLIELMO, *Crucifix*, Duomo, Sarzana

Fig. 2 - LUCCAN MASTER, *The Servi Crucifix*, Pinacoteca, Lucca

Fig. 3 - BERLINGHIERO BERLINGHIERI, *Crucifix*, Pinacoteca, Lucca

Fig. 4 - MASTER OF THE OBLATE CRUCIFIX, *Crucifix*, Oblate Convent, Florence

versally great art of Cimabue, the Master of San Martino, or Duccio di Buoninsegna did not, of course, spring from a void. It presupposed the art of Giunta Pisano and his circle — or rather, the particular way of interpreting Byzantine culture that is characteristic of Duecento Tuscan painters and which distinguishes them from, say, the contemporaneous Balkan and Russian masters of the icon.

The Tuscan painters of the Duecento were also, in a sense, masters of the icon (and so they well might appear from the point of view of the Western Romanesque period), but their common bond lies in their aspirations and modes of expression, derived from an opposite shore — the Byzantine East. This allegiance with Eastern art is scant reason for censuring their art, especially if it is founded on the basis of a tradition that the painters and their patrons did not even know or, possibly, may have rejected.

Instead, let us view this art in relation to the figurative tradition that inspired and nourished it. The grandeur and magnitude of the Byzantine tradition places it high in the history of human endeavor. Considered in this light, we must marvel at the spirit of independence and extraordinary inventiveness that, within their confines, Tuscan painters brought about, adding new dimensions that reflected their own Western mentality. The fact that, as Victor Lazarev observed, their works are modeled on the modest productions of outlying provinces, from Macedonia and Armenia to Cappodocia, instead of on the more eminent ones of Constantinople in no way diminishes their worth. The Tuscan genius breathed new life into the formulas borrowed from those cultures that had grown stale in stifling conventions; and what, by any standards, seemed destined to remain the most marginal of Byzantium's extended glories instead provided its central and most conclusive moment; from it springs the miracle of Cimabue and Duccio.

Medieval Tuscan painters also made an outstanding contribution in the creation and refinement of completely new iconographic themes, which either were unknown or differently treated in Eastern painting. The principal and most prevalent of these is the theme of the Crucifixion, painted on variously shaped panels, with or without accompanying scenes from the Passion. There are two versions: the Christus Triumphans (the still-living Christ) and the Christus Patiens (the dead or dying Christ). There is reason to believe that the painted Crucifix is a Tuscan invention. The earliest known example of these — a Crucifix (fig. 1) in the Cathedral of Sarzana, dated 1138 and signed by a certain Master Guglielmo, who probably was Luccan — is Tuscan, and the greatest number of this type, with the widest variety of iconographic formulations, is to be found in Tuscany. The Tuscan painter Giunta Pisano is the first one we know to have portrayed the Christus Patiens on a panel.

Numerous types of altar frontals and altarpieces appeared shortly after the painted Crucifix; they are either vertical or horizontal in structure, with a large central figure flanked by a series of scenes. The earliest and greatest number of examples are Tuscan and differ considerably from the famous Romanesque antependia of Catalonia; they are found in Pisa, Arezzo, Siena, Lucca, and Florence. A painter who wanted to illustrate scenes from the Passion of Christ at the sides of a Crucifix, or scenes from the life of Mary alongside a Madonna, often found ready-made iconographic schemes in Byzantine miniatures and frescoes. Then again, he might be depicting events and miracles in the lives of contemporary saints or of those who, for other reasons, were unknown in the Eastern

Fig. 5 - BONAVENTURA BERLINGHIERI, *Saint Francis of Assisi Between Two Angels, and Six Scenes from His Life,* Church of San Francesco, Pescia

liturgy. The prime example is Saint Francis of Assisi, for whom iconographic motifs were created in thirteenth-century Tuscan workshops.

Any medium of expression capable of such widespread influence, of responding to the aesthetic, religious, and social exigencies of such a vital and highly sophisticated Western society certainly should not be called anachronistic. Similarly, so far as painting is concerned, Tuscany before the appearance of Cimabue cannot be called "a land without history, and for the time being incapable of producing any." For one thing, this statement is refuted by Tuscany's ready and wide response — the first such response in Italy — to the new influences emanating from Byzantium soon after the fall of Constantinople in 1204. Other types of influence also must have received welcome in Tuscany, since Duecento Tuscan painting cannot possibly be mistaken for the work of any province in the Balkans, Asia Minor, Russia, or, even more simply, Southern Italy, despite the fact that, though they were fundamentally opposed, the Romanesque and Byzantine worlds had definite links, and any line of demarcation between them is extremely hazy.

The amazing variety of artistic characteristics produced in thirteenth-century Tuscan painting makes any distinctions of a geographic or regional nature inadequate and hopelessly generic. We can disregard the exact place of execution or more general province for individual works and still find standards of distinction and classification in their stylistic indications. Stylistic analysis, to a greater degree than geographical criteria, corresponds to the historical situation of medieval Tuscany, where each of the great centers had its own tradition and its own school. These centers were Lucca, Pisa, Siena, Florence, and, to a lesser degree, Arezzo; their mutual contacts and interdependencies do not obscure the basic and unmistakable individuality of their principal manifestations. We now shall turn to these centers for a brief survey of artistic developments in twelfth-century Tuscany.

Lucca, formerly the seat of a powerful Longobard dukedom and the principal city of Tuscany during the eleventh and twelfth centuries, takes chronological precedence in the history of Tuscan painting. The Luccan school had its solemn inception with the previously mentioned Crucifix (fig. 1), signed and dated 1138 by Master Guglielmo; it probably came from Luni and is now in the Duomo at Sarzana. The head and torso of Christ were repainted about a century later, but examination by X ray has shown that the later artist kept to the original iconographic scheme, a Romanesque Christus Triumphans probably derived from Carolingian ivories. The tabellone (panels below the arms of the cross, flanking the Corpus) represents Saint John and the Madonna weeping, accompanied by two holy women, and six scenes from the Passion. The capicroci (panels at the ends of the arms) contain symbols of the Evangelists and the prophets Jeremiah and Isaiah, and the finial shows the Ascension. This work has been compared stylistically to a number of somewhat later paintings from Latium, such as the famous triptych (plate 34) in the Duomo at Tivoli and the *Crucifixion* at Casape near Tivoli, to which we might add the earlier *Vetralla Madonna*. However, the Lucca *Crucifixion* differs from these in its breadth of inspiration and a vigorous incisiveness that strikes an accent of Romanesque plasticity in the majestic image of Christ and imbues the minor figures and scenes with raw dramatic immediacy.

Guglielmo came from Lucca or, at least, was trained there, as is shown by a comparison of the style of his established work, substantially more Romanesque than Byzantine, with that of the numerous illuminated manuscripts produced in the largely Benedictine

14

Figs. 6 & 7 - Master of the Oblate Crucifix, *Diptych*, Galleria dell'Accademia, Florence

monasteries of the Luccan region. Guglielmo's art must have attracted a large following in Lucca; during the second half of the twelfth century we still find Crucifixes plainly patterned on the Sarzana Crucifix. Two of these — one in San Michele at Pisa and one formerly in Santa Maria dei Servi, now in the Lucca Pinacoteca — were probably painted by one man. He gives Guglielmo a refined and polished interpretation, both in the elegant subtlety of the design (particularly in the scenes, which are no longer crowded together but gracefully spread out) and the exquisitely delicate range of colors, dominated by gentle tones of ash blue. The Servi Crucifix (fig. 2) aspires toward clear and ordered composition, producing a strongly rhythmic and decorative effect. This also appears in the symmetrical consistency among the scenes, with their lively actors and fragile architecture sharply defined against a gold background. The body of the San Michele Christ is modeled with slight relief in stucco, as occurs also in several Sienese paintings of the early Duecento. In both Crucifixes, the face of Christ is beginning to lose its impassive, abstract expression and is veiled in a quite human look of sadness. The head rests lightly on the right shoulder.

This anonymous artist, perhaps the greatest of twelfth-century Tuscan painters, was followed by the painter of the *Crucifixion* in the Church of Santa Giulia in Lucca. This artist dates from the third or fourth decade of the thirteenth century and his works have the unmistakable stamp of Berlinghiero's Byzantine style. Berlinghiero was the head of a family of painters that included his sons Bonaventura, Marco, and Barone. Berlinghiero is mentioned in a document of 1228 and died before 1248. Believed, mistakenly, to be of Milanese origin, his name is found at the bottom of a Crucifix (fig. 3) formerly located in Santa Maria degli Angioli, now in the Lucca Pinacoteca. Berlinghiero's Crucifix is much smaller than the preceding ones. Instead of scenes on the tabellone, there are only figures of the sorrowing Virgin and Saint John. The painting shows a greater understanding of Byzantine art — possibly that of the provinces as opposed to that of Constantinople — but the figurative characteristics remain essentially Western and Romanesque in nature. In the light of successive cultural developments in local painting, it would be wrong to interpret these characteristics as signs of a renaissance; they are merely survivors of a world already transformed into art by Guglielmo and the Master of the Servi and San Michele Crucifix. None of Barone Berlinghiero's works are extant, and his brother Marco is credited only with a mediocre *Crucifixion* in Santa Maria Assunta at Villa Basilica. Unlike that of his father, Bonaventura's work shows the Byzantine style gaining the upper hand over Romanesque tendencies (then again, these had appeared on the scene so recently that they barely show up in the work of Guglielmo and his followers, not to speak of constituting a genuine and separate tradition), but we cannot agree with the recent contention that in Bonaventura the Byzantine style froze into crabbed and stillborn formulations. He is mentioned in Luccan documents from 1228 to 1274, and his only known work is the altarpiece (fig. 5), *Saint Francis of Assisi Between Two Angels, and Six Scenes from His Life*, signed and dated 1235, in the Church of San Francesco at Pescia. Of central importance in the history of Franciscan iconography, this altarpiece used to enjoy an excessive reputation. Nowadays it is difficult to view the painting as "an ideal representation of Saint Francis, far superior to the majority of later more famous paintings" or to appreciate its "intrinsic mysticism that could never be achieved through mere description, however skillfully executed" (Osvald Sirén); still, we cannot ignore its freshness of invention and singular purity of expression, which, especially in the flanking scenes, applied the Byzantine graphic conventions with such narrative deftness that the old mannerisms seem to come alive once again. Like the earlier Servi Crucifix, this tabellone's outstanding quality is its well-balanced, spacious composition; while the six scenes are well set off from one another, the rhythm of the composition relates the characters in an expressive byplay that adds interest to their immobile features. The central figure with its exaggerated length appears to frame the whole like an architectural accent.

Several works that have been grouped together with the Pescia altarpiece also are ascribed often to Bonaventura. One of these, a Crucifix (fig. 4) in the Oblate Convent in Florence, is outstanding in quality. In addition to the pensive, moving figures of the two mourners on the tabellone, its smoothly modeled forms and luminous colors seem direct echoes of Berlinghiero, although the iconographic scheme of Christus Patiens surely is taken from Pisan models. Its pronounced yet supple design is a far cry from Bonaventura's arid style. Disregarding the stylistic evidence, this superb master's Luccan origin seems to be confirmed by another work that comes from Lucca's Convent of Santa Chiara and can securely be attributed to him. This diptych (plates 2 and 3; figs. 6 and 7) in the Florentine Accademia displays *The Madonna and Child Surrounded by Eight Saints* on one panel and the *Crucifixion with Four Scenes from the Passion* on the other. Unless the figure of Saint Clare was added later by a different hand, the fact that she was canonized in 1255 makes her presence in the Accademia diptych proof that the Master of the Oblate Crucifix was active through the middle of the thirteenth century. In his work we find the close of the true Luccan tradition in painting. Those few artists that continue to echo its forms in rustic and provincial versions do not really enter into our discussion, and it has no link with the graceful but minor work of Deodato Orlandi. Orlandi was active between the close of the Duecento and the first two decades of the Trecento; formed in the style of Cimabue and, in part, Seneseggio, his development shows the first intimations of Giotto's approaching thunder.

A group of Crucifixions marks the beginning of painting in the School of Pisa. Some of these — for example, the Accademia Crucifix (plates 1, 4, and 5) and the one in the Parrochiale of Rosano (fig. 8) — are found around Florence, which leads to some question as to whether the group is entirely Pisan; it is agreed that those that might have been painted in Florence are very closely related to those definitely Pisan in origin, among which the *Crucifixion* in the Church of San Frediano is the oldest of the group. The Christus Patiens motif and the scenes obviously are styled after Master Guglielmo's Sarzana *Crucifixion*. The scenes, however, already show signs of the divergent tendencies that begin to distinguish Pisan from Luccan painting. They have increased in number and are completely independent of the main figure. Thus, a marked taste for story telling and illustration appears early as characteristic of Pisan painting. This fondness for narration and sometimes vivid dramatization is the main element in the Pisan primitives' particular style and forms the basis of the brief but intense period of the Pisan Romanesque that preceded the great surge of Duecento Byzantinism. The strictly Western quality of several of the scenes in the San Frediano Crucifix has been brought out a number of times (primarily by Vavalà), as has the exceptional nature or rarity (for instance, the *Resurrection*) of some of them. These constitute sure evidence of the artist's innovating spirit and the correspondingly open and liberal atmosphere in which he worked. Even those actions distantly patterned on the repertory of Byzantine, Syrian, or Cappadocian stylized gestures are charged with such spontaneous vitality that they seem created for the occasion. Their smoothly rounded or abrupt outlines animate the cramped space of the individual scenes, which are composed with the utmost rhythmical freedom and with architectural and scenic elements reduced to a minimum.

Even this amount of freedom appears somewhat restricted compared to that of the Crucifix in the Parrocchiale of Rosano near Pontassieve (Florence). The two paintings are so alike stylistically that some critics attribute them to the same hand, but despite its freer use of Byzantine iconographic schemes and motifs, the linear course of the Rosano Crucifix is more fluent, rapid, and vibrant. Now curving smoothly, now bounding ahead with darting impetuosity, it tells a wonderful story of the anonymous painter's passionate engagement in the drama of Christ. When confronted by such mastery of line — the most fundamental means of expression — one can hardly

Fig. 8 - PISAN MASTER (?), *Crucifix* (detail), Parrocchiale Church, Rosano (Florence)

speak of primitivism or mistake pure and open simplicity for crudeness or lack of skill. While its graphic origins remain evident, the transition from manuscripts patiently wrought in the monastery scriptoria to the plastered and gilt panels of the painters' workshops has enabled line to gain new potentials of form synthesis and an almost tangible quintessence and purity.

The so-called Accademia Crucifix, now in the Uffizi in Florence, is related in type and iconography to the San Frediano and Rosano Crucifixes. Defined as one of the masterpieces of medieval Italy, this famous work is of unknown origin. It emerges from the same cultural ambiance as the San Frediano and Rosano Crucifixes but tends in a different direction, showing greater and more elusive complexity of color and design. The flushed and heavy tones of the two preceding Crucifixes are replaced by delicate, translucent shades of pink, lilac, and clear blue, a choice suggestive of Spoleto's Crucifixes and the very earliest Sienese panels and seldom encountered previously. If this does reflect the Umbrian and Sienese palette, we are given a means for dating the Accademia Crucifix somewhere around the last decade of the twelfth century or very early in the thirteenth century. The unusual choice of color corresponds to an extremely clean and precise design. The line is less mobile than in the Rosano scenes; the figures are blocked in with firm strokes. Their highlighted garments are painstakingly draped in minute folds over bodies that seem a bit dwarfed by their large heads. The characters' energetic and elegant gestures serve to heighten the feverish intensity that their facial expressions give to the scenes. They peer at one another from the corners of their dark and shallow-set eyes in a flickering network of heavy-browed glances that express the feelings of the actors in the drama with startling forcefulness. Yet the poetry of the passion expressed in this striking Crucifix is deeply, serenely elegiac. It must have been painted by a highly cultivated artist who, in addition to local and Umbro-Roman traditions, draws upon those from the distant provinces of Byzantium, especially Armenia and Syria. A recent study has established connections between this Crucifix and several frescoes dating from between the end of the

18

twelfth century and the early thirteenth century and located at Barletta in the Church of San Sepolcro. This is good evidence of its Pisan origin, in view of the frequent contact and parallel cultural developments existing between the regions of Pisa and Apulia.

This initial group of Pisan paintings is characterized by the adoption of Western Romanesque iconographic motifs and that known as the Living Christ (Christus Triumphans). Its most abundantly illustrated Crucifix (plates 6 and 7) comes from the Church of San Sepolcro and is number fifteen in Pisa's Museo Nazionale di San Matteo. It includes no less than ten scenes, one of which is in two parts: the *Journey* and the *Supper at Emmaus*. This does not necessarily make it last in line of succession among these Crucifixes discussed above. Its richly developed illustrative apparatus and certain more markedly Byzantine characteristics (greater airiness of composition, a fondness for symmetry, and the introduction of new iconographic motifs) would tend to place it later than the San Frediano, Rosano, and Accademia Crucifixes, it reflects to a greater degree than these the very earliest phase of Pisan miniatures, which reached a high point in an 1168–69 Bible in Calci's Carthusian Monastery. The San Sepolcro Crucifix is painted in lively colors, which are splendidly preserved, and the scenes have a clear and effective order; but delightful as these are, the painting reveals the touch of an artist much narrower in sensitivity than the masters of the San Frediano, Rosano, and Accademia Crucifixes. We might term it the work of a diligent artisan who hammers away at the same stony-faced characters, which share the mannered quality of figures in an illuminated manuscript.

The *Crucifixion* (plate 8; fig. 26), originally from the Monastery of San Matteo, is a much finer work. It is technically unusual, being painted on a piece of parchment that has been fixed to the panel. Critics, with few exceptions, extol its high quality and recognize its cast as primarily Byzantine. "A sort of Comnenes miniature on a giant scale, with minute brush work dazzlingly executed" (F. Bologna), its Pisan origin nonetheless is vouched for by its exact duplication of iconographic motifs found in corresponding scenes of the San Frediano and San Sepolcro Crucifixes. The cursive style of design also is similar to these works. The figure of Christ attempts to combine the new iconographic motif of the Byzantine Christus Patiens with the traditional Luccan Christus Triumphans scheme of composition. The hybrid result shows a Christ beyond the point of suffering. This new version of a dead Christ was transitory in nature and produced no successors.

A certain awkward stiffness of execution can be imputed to the difficulty of reconciling the new, more aulic Byzantine modes with pre-existing schemes. It is, in fact, most glaring in the figure of Christ. This wooden quality is practically unnoticeable when the painter adheres more closely to his splendid metropolitan Byzantine models or gives free access to their aura of delicate pathos, as occurs in the scenes; the dramatic and active episodes of the Passion are passed over in favor of the poignancy of the *Death* and *Entombment*. The jutting line of a colonnade, the fleeting rhythms of arches and Eastern cupolas sharply depicted against an antique gold background join with the curved and elegant outlines of the figures in producing a musical flow of space. The conventional graphic treatment of the characters does not lessen the genuine feeling that pervades the most touching moments of this ancient grief, which here is given the miracle of new life.

This admirable Crucifix probably dates from the second or third decade of the

19

Fig. 9 - GIUNTA PISANO, *Crucifix* (detail), Church of San Domenico, Bologna

thirteenth century. It was recently suggested that these dates be revised backwards, in keeping with a theory that the work was the catalyst for a supposed change in Giunta Pisano's style. This suggestion, which must be treated with great reservation, reflects the theory of those critics who regard Giunta's formation as stemming from the San Matteo Crucifix. Giunta Capitani, known as Giunta Pisano, is the first painter for whom there are records in the town archives of Pisa. He is mentioned in documents from 1229 to 1254. He signed three Crucifixes, those in the Church of Santa Maria degli Angioli in Assisi (fig. 10), San Raniero in Pisa, and San Domenico in Bologna (fig. 9). His name and the date 1236 appeared on a Crucifix, later destroyed in the thirteenth century, commissioned by Brother Elias for the Basilica of San Francesco in Assisi. Giunta's artistic formation, instead of depending on the San Matteo Crucifix, seems to stem rather from Berlinghiero's interpretation of so-called Byzantine neo-Hellenism. Berlinghiero, who was from Lucca, died before 1242 and was perhaps somewhat older than his colleague from Pisa. This is not to say that Berlinghiero's Byzantinism may not itself have been of Pisan origin, because of Pisa's well-known contact with countries beyond the sea. The point is that Berlinghiero and Giunta both possess a broader and more timely understanding of Byzantine culture than we find in the painter of the San Matteo Crucifix. Perhaps portable mosaics were more responsible than the art of the miniaturist or the goldsmith in starting them toward the purest and most intense painting in late-Comnene or pre-Paleologue art.

Giunta Pisano deserves the credit for a complete transformation of the concept of the painted Crucifix, establishing a tradition that remains the model during the whole Duecento and beyond. He does away with the narrative scenes of earlier Crucifixes and confines the figures of the Virgin and Saint John to the end pieces (capricroce) of the horizontal arms. Giunta's Crucifixions are not repetitions of the pure emblems or symbols of those in the first days of Christian civilization; neither are they meant to be realistic representations of the supreme event in the Divine Tragedy. The sublime originality of

20

Fig. 10 - GIUNTA PISANO, *Crucifix*, Church of Santa Maria degli Angioli, Assisi

Giunta's concept transcends the limits of reality in representing a dead Jesus whose limbs arch and strain upward as if gripped in a final spasm of agony, instead of hanging limply from the Cross. Surely, the new image of Christ as man's brother in suffering that Saint Francis had nurtured in the hearts of the multitude found depths of response in the bitter eloquence of such a portrayal.

The chronological order of Giunta's signed Crucifixes has been established for some time on the basis of compelling morphological differences. (The Assisi Crucifix would be the oldest, the San Raniero the next, and then the Bologna Crucifix.) This order has given rise to diverse and sometimes contradictory interpretations of the painter's stylistic development, which plainly shows the progressive and intimate coming to maturity in the artist's vision, in connection with the conscious refinement of his methods. The somewhat rough and analytical treatment of anatomy in the Assisi Crucifix is replaced by the eloquent articulations of the San Raniero Christ's violently curved body; the Bologna Crucifix approaches a synthesis in form and an all-encompassing singleness of vision, the almost monumental grandeur which is beyond the need for the nervous type of line that informs the San Raniero Crucifix in sudden, rushing surges. The curvature of the Bologna Christ's body is less emphasized than the San Raniero Christ, but equally pure and unbroken. The organic treatment of the body articulation and the swift definition of the limbs (lightly tapered by masterful shading along the sides) is commanded by an even subtler sense of continuous line.

Such development is wrongly defined in terms of a transition from the dramatic to the cathartic, or vice versa. We actually are dealing with different shades of a single feeling, of a basically unchanged emotional attitude that is seeking more coherent means of expression through a constant purification of form and more exacting standards of beauty.

Giunta's vast influence — not only in Pisa but throughout those parts of Umbria and Emilia in which he worked — is shown by a great number of Crucifixes, some of which are attributed to Giunta himself; one of the finest examples is the small processional Cross (plate 9; fig. 28) formerly in the Vallombrosa Monastery and now in the Pisa Museum. But — not to lose ourselves in a labyrinth of unsigned works — the direct line of Giunta's influence is perhaps best traced in the work of Ugolino di Tedice (mentioned in documents of 1273 and 1277, this painter signed a moving Crucifixion now in the Leningrad Hermitage Museum), and in the work of his son Ranieri di Ugolino. The latter's *Crucifixion* is number seventeen in the Pisa Museum; despite its lamentable state of preservation, we catch glimpses of a once great dramatic power.

Ugolino di Tedice's brother, Enrico di Tedice, is mentioned in a document of 1254. To judge from the single painting that at one time preserved his signature — a *Crucifixion* (fig. 11) in the Church of San Martino in Pisa — Enrico, unlike Ugolino, represents a trend in Pisan painting that developed independently of Giunta toward the middle of the thirteenth century. Because this approach combines an extremely free touch with violent expressiveness, some critics have termed it impressionistic, others expressionistic; in less anachronistic terms, it is a spontaneous and synthesizing development of certain pre-existing tendencies. Enrico di Tedice must have had some contact with certain Byzantine provincial styles, perhaps through miniature art and Pisa, which opened onto the ports-of-call in the Balkan East. The contrast between the unspoiled and simple expressivity of these

22

Fig. 11 - ENRICO DI TEDICE, *The Entombment* and *The Three Marys at the Sepulchre* (detail from a Crucifix), Church of San Martino, Pisa

provincial forms and the aristocratic metropolitan art of the Comnenes is evident in the murals adorning the rock-hewn chapels of Cappadocia and frescoes in Serbian, Greek, and Macedonian churches, as well as in the provincial mosaic.

The well-illustrated tabellone of the San Martino Crucifix reflects the pre-Giunta school. A coursing impetus of line is characteristic and, especially in the scenes, produces raw-edged dramatic effects that barely stop short of the grotesque. It also is distinguished by delicate, gemlike colors, quickened by flickering highlights of white lead. The same elements are handled with greater finesse in an exquisite miniature panel *Descent from the Cross*, number fourteen in the Pisa Museum, which some critics add to Enrico's works. *Saint Catherine of Alexandria with Eight Scenes from Her Life* (plates 10 and 11), an altarpiece from the Church of San Silvestro and now in the Pisa Museum, usually is placed in the same vein of painting. It has a certain impromptu quality, a freshness of touch, primarily in the scenes, that is inspired by impressionistic Byzantine miniatures; this, and the lively narrative simplicity of a folk tale, provides some analogy with the San Martino Crucifix. But a different hand is apparent in the latter's stress on plastic form, which likens it to contemporary products of the Florentine school.

During the last half of the Duecento, the give and take between Pisan and Florentine painting (and, subordinately, between Pisan and Sienese painting) became progressively closer and more intense, until we come across works that are stylistically on the borderline between the two schools. An example is *Saint Verano and Six Scenes from His Life*, a panel in Milan's Gerli collection that probably came from Peccioli; another is the excellent dossale, number three in the Pisa Museum, formerly in the Church of San Silvestro. This leads us to believe that Pisa was the direct Byzantine source for Coppo di Marcovaldo, who was the top Florentine painter before Cimabue; and the so-called Master of San Martino, who, without question, was Pisa's major painter, is clearly in debt to Coppo for the Byzantine aspects of his work. The Pisan Master takes his name from a panel (plates 12–14; fig. 12) in the Pisa Museum that comes from the Church of San Martino. It shows the *Enthroned Madonna and Child* flanked by ten scenes; below the throne is a representation of Saint Martin giving his cloak to the beggar. Another panel (plate 15) in the Pisa Museum with *Saint Anne, Enthroned, Holding the Young Madonna* is universally attributed to the same Master. It also is likely that a *Madonna* in the Acton collection in Florence belongs to the period of his late activity, as Longhi correctly suggests.

The cultural breadth of this great painter (who also was a miniaturist, as shown in several splendid illustrations of an Exultet Roll in the Pisa Museum that are unmistakably by his hand) is widely inclusive in time and extent. It not only ranges from the aristocratic forms of the old Byzantine convention found in painters like Giunta to the impressionistic painting of an Enrico di Tedice, but beautifully picks up the classical element latent in the works of sculptors like Guglielmo and Bonnaro, and which finds its dazzling epiphany in the works of Nicola Pisano. Thus he is comprehensive, and in some sense conclusive, of the highest local tradition. Nor does he ignore the vigorous plastic abstract-monumentalism of Coppo di Marcovaldo; and far from Tuscany, he reaches out feelers toward the precocious Gothic style of Frederick II's imperial workshops. The Master of San Martino, active between the seventh and eighth decades of the Duecento, completes the cycle of medieval painting at Pisa and at the same time opens a new and fundamental

24

Fig. 12 - MASTER OF SAN MARTINO, *Enthroned Madonna and Child and Ten Scenes from the Legend of Anne and Joachim*, Museo Nazionale di San Matteo, Pisa

chapter in the history of Italian painting. Its finest pages will be penned at Siena by the masters preceding Duccio di Buoninsegna, by Duccio himself, and, above all, by Cimabue at Florence.

Arezzo's painting activity is centered almost exclusively around a single artist. Margherito di Magnano (better known as Margaritone d'Arezzo) is mentioned in a document of 1262. Arezzo's earlier activity is represented by a number of Christus Triumphans Crucifixes resembling Berlinghiero's in type but close in style to the interpretation of Luccan modes as used by early Florentine painters such as the Master of Bigallo. Margaritone, too, starts out from the Master of Bigallo; but he also was familiar with Pisa's more mannered and parched forms of Byzantinism, a perfect example of which is the panel of *Saint Francis Accompanied by Scenes from His Life* in the Church of San Francesco. Margaritone's version of Pisan formulas has a singularly archaic cast, evident in the marked frontality of the figures and the spare, almost heraldic composition of the scenes. Something of the spontaneous vitality of folklore characters

Fig. 13 - GUIDO DA SIENA, *Maestà* (detail), Palazzo Pubblico, Siena

bursts through the rigid contours of his rather scrawny and stunted-looking characters; the results are far superior to their courtly models. We can best point to his many portrayals of Saint Francis (plate 16); several quite similar versions are known, five of them signed. The Saint's features are a bit harsh, but his great eyes engage our own, and the gestures beckoning gently from the confines of the narrow panel seem to invite a warmer contact with the viewer than, for example, Bonaventura Berlinghieri's gloomy and forbidding hermit or the calligraphic grace of the aristocratic figure in the famous panel in Assisi's Santa Maria degli Angioli. We also can turn to his figures of the Madonna, found in the Montelugano and Washington Icons, or, surrounded by scenes, in the signed dossali from Arezzo in London's National Gallery and the Sanctuary of the Vertighe near San Savino. The Madonnas are as isolated by their heavy outlines as the figures in Central Italian carvings: if not

exactly counterparts, they surely
seem the painted equivalents of
these wood figures. Completely
lacking in sweetness as they are,
the tension contained in the Madonna's watchful expressions and
pensive gestures appears on the
verge of shattering that hieratic
impassiveness.

Duecento painting at Siena
developed much later than at Lucca or Pisa, but the results were
well worth the waiting. The oldest
paintings of any type discovered
in Sienese territory are three Crucifixions dating between the end of
the twelfth century to the early
thirteenth century. One, from the
church in San Giovanni d'Asso, is
in the Siena Pinacoteca, another
in the Museo di Arte in Montalci-
no, and the third, a slightly later
painting, is in the Siena Pinacoteca. We cannot be sure whether
these represent an indigenous tradition or, instead, are reflections
of the school of Spoleto. The

Fig. 14 - GUIDO DA SIENA, *The Redeemer Giving Blessing* (detail from the *Maestà*)

Crucifixions are Romanesque in style and are painted in light tones with liberal use
of azure blue, which also is characteristic of an altar frontal depicting *The Redeemer
Enthroned, and Six Scenes from the History of the True Cross* (dated 1215, it comes
from the Cloister at Ardenga and is now in the Siena Pinacoteca); the main figures and
decorative details framing the scenes are executed in relief, the same procedure followed
in an *Enthroned Madonna* (known as the *Madonna with Large Eyes*) located in the
Museo dell'Opera del Duomo di Siena, and once the central section of a dossale that
seems originally to have included scenes. The elements common to the works mentioned,
and to others either derived from these or of minor importance, may not be sufficient
to establish the existence of a bona fide Sienese school of painting in the last decades of
the thirteenth century. But the various treatments in the individual works, indicating
distinct artistic personalities, does not hide their fundamental unity of approach and
cultural background. Of particular interest is the fact that their development was independent of either preceding or contemporary Tuscan movements and, instead, was linked
with developments in Umbria and Latium.

Guido da Siena, as he is called, is the first Sienese painter whose name we know and
whose works are extant. Guido signed a huge Maestà panel, originally in the Church of

San Domenico and now in the Palazzo Pubblico — including a Maestà (fig. 13), with *The Redeemer* (fig. 14) on its cusp — bearing the date 1221. Definitive research shows this date to be inaccurate (it probably refers to an earlier work, to which the present one roughly corresponds), since many of the painting's historical and stylistic elements prevent it from being any earlier than the seventh decade of the century, and the influence of Coppo di Marcovaldo and, possibly, Migliore (who were both in Siena after the battle of Montaperti in 1260) is obvious here as in other panels generally attributed to Guido. The disciple outshines his two masters, however, in a monumental and spacious composition; the conceptual breadth of Guido's *Enthroned Madonna* more than equals the outsize dimensions of the painting, which achieves a solemn majesty new not only in Tuscan painting but in the whole range of panel painting in Italy. Unfortunately, the centrally important Madonna, Child, and throne were repainted in the very early Trecento by an excellent follower of Duccio or, possibly, by Duccio himself. We achieve an idea of the original by studying the altarpiece's perfectly preserved cusp and by examination of the corresponding parts in his other panels, primarily a fragmentary *Madonna and Child* (plate 17) in the Siena Pinacoteca. When still intact, this painting bore the date 1262. Probably painted several years earlier than the Palazzo Pubblico *Maestà* (such is the name given portrayals of the Madonna and Child or the Saviour receiving homage from saints and angels), it already shows leanings toward a break with Byzantine graphic conventions (which Coppo had twisted into a semblance of plasticity) and into more fluent and subtle modes of expression. A dossale with the mutilated date 127– in the Siena Pinacoteca also tends in this direction.

Although Guido observes the iconographic canons and graphic formalities of the Greek style to the letter, his refined execution and the clean, well-balanced spacing of his colors show a strikingly individual approach. The huge areas of color are bounded by firm, incisive outlines free of any rigidity and livened by a dazzling play of gold highlights. The colors are exquisite — brilliant when vivid, but more often blended and shaded in masterful intonations. The composition unfolds in stately cadence; the forms are delicately wrought. The technical treatment is matched by an equally new and compelling quality of mind, an intimate tenderness that restores the guise of naturalness and a very human sense of foreboding to the impassive masks of the Byzantine Madonnas. This sweet quality anticipates much of the Sienese art that followed. Guido's are also the gentlest of all Duecento Madonnas; one immediately thinks of the 1262 *Madonna*, which is one of the surest, most meaningful, and well preserved. A recent appraisal of the Master of Saint Martin easily could apply to Guido's portrayal of the Madonna: "In the medieval process of humanization, they bring the discovery of a common language one step closer" (Bologna). This is equally true if Guido's humanistic disposition should happen to be psychological in origin, rather than a product of lucid appraisal of the problems that the now fossilized Byzantine usages were posing for the artists of the time who were most aware.

The many works produced by his immediate circle show that Guido's surroundings were alive to the possibilities of a renaissance. Among these works are some scenes from the *Life and Passion of Christ* that at one time formed the wings, or hinged side panels, of the *Maestà* (five are in the Siena Pinacoteca; others are found at Altenberg, Utrecht, Princeton, and Lausanne) and a unique tabellone of the *Last Judgment* in the Grosseto

Fig. 15 - MIGLIORE, *The Redeemer, Flanked by the Virgin and Saints Peter, John the Evangelist, and Paul*, Galleria dell'Accademia, Florence

Museum. A more exciting indication would be the possibility that Guido himself painted such a genuine masterpiece as the dossale (plates 18 and 19; figs. 32 and 33), *Saint Peter, Enthroned, Flanked by Six Scenes* in the Siena Pinacoteca; the attribution may be difficult to prove but certainly deserves attention. Here, Guido's artistic language comes into its own, finding its loftiest expression in an intelligent and bold alliance with Cimabue's style.

This highly sophisticated movement was open to the latest developments in Florence and Pisa and a definite correlative — if not an actual component — of Duccio's formation. But side by side there was developing a less aulic version of the elements inherited from Guido, one with a strongly popular flavor and represented by the so-called Master of the Blessed Gallerani, author of two hinged diptychs (plates 22 and 23) in the Siena Pinacoteca portraying scenes from the life of the Blessed Andrea Gallerani and four saints. What the two lack in the way of color and technique is redeemed by their straightforward intensity of expression and jaunty style of recounting the scenes with an unspoiled richness of realistic details.

We do not know exactly where a certain Vigoroso da Siena fits into the context of Sienese painting, if indeed he belongs there at all. He was strongly influenced by Coppo and Cimabue, as seen in his one known work, a polyptych dated 1282 or 1283 in the Perugia Pinacoteca. A similar lack of knowledge surrounds the author of a *Crucifixion* in the San Gimignano Museum, also influenced by Cimabue. A superb frontal (plates 20 and 21) in the Siena Pinacoteca of *Saint John the Baptist* accompanied by *Twelve Scenes from His Life* stands out against this background, but there is no doubt about its Sienese origin; for "Duccio himself was not indifferent to its appearance" (Brandi), and Brandi and Zerli recently credited its painter with a *Saint Francis and Four Scenes from His Life* in the Cathedral at Orte. Definitely a later work than the altar frontal, and with several motifs derived from Guido's circle, the *Saint Francis* is proof that its painter worked at Siena. The altar frontal creates a separate problem in the context of Tuscan painting as a whole, being so strongly and directly influenced by Byzantine paintings and miniatures of the so-called second golden age. This is leading to general acceptance of the hypothesis that

29

this unique panel was painted by an artist trained in miniatures, as reflected in the iconography of the scenes — crowded with round-towers, varicolored cupolas, and girdling battlements — and in the very choice of colors: primarily rich, heavy reds, cobalts, and ochers — neatly alternated and contrasted in a way that reminds us of an Oriental illuminated manuscript. All this lies outside the Tuscan tradition but is well within its range of cultural receptivity. Thus Siena, the last Tuscan city to come under the dominance of the so-called Greek style, was also the one to develop its purest and most intense manifestations and, above all, that was able to turn them into a fertile groundwork for the future developments in her school.

The cultural components of Florentine painting came from various directions. From the middle of the twelfth century on, there was a flourishing miniaturistic tradition, but the first painters to work at Florence or send her their products probably were not native Florentines. The painters of the Accademia and Rosano Crucifixes were in fact Pisan, and the Master of the Oblate Crucifix was Luccan. Fra Jacopo di San Francesco, who shortly after 1228 created the mosaic for the scarsella, or pulpit, of the Baptistry of San Giovanni, is of uncertain provenance — perhaps Roman or Umbrian. There is even a suspicion that the Master of Bigallo came from Pisa. This Master takes his name from a *Crucifixion* in the Bigallo Museum; the painting's execution has been tied in with the 1224 founding of the Confraternity. Richard Offner's study (1933) of the Master's artistic personality attributes to him several works — among others, the Madonnas in the Montalvo Conservatory, Florence's Acton collection, the Museum of Nantes, and Pittsburgh's Hahn collection, and a dossale (fig. 16), *Saint Zenobius and Four Scenes from His Life* in the Museo dell'Opera del Duomo in Florence. His manner, derived from Berlinghiero, has certain affinities with that of Margaritone d'Arezzo; it has yet to be decided whether Margaritone was influenced by the Master of Bigallo or vice versa. In any case, his style's evolving emphasis on plastic form is analogous to the development followed by Margaritone and other Florentine painters with whom Bigallo had definite contact, such as the Master of the Bardi Saint Francis.

The Master of the Bardi Saint Francis painted the large panel (plates 24 and 25; fig. 35) *Saint Francis of Assisi with Twenty Scenes from His Life* in the Bardi Chapel of

Fig. 16 - MASTER OF BIGALLO, *Saint Zenobius and Four Scenes from His Life*, Museo dell'Opera del Duomo, Florence

Fig. 17 - MIGLIORE, *Madonna and Child, Flanked by Saints Peter and Paul and Four Scenes from Their Lives*, Church of San Leolino, Panzano (Florence)

the Church of Santa Croce in Florence and a *Crucifixion with Eight Scenes* in the Uffizi Gallery. He too has close connections with the Berlinghieros, particularly Bonaventura; it even has been suggested that the Bardi Master is none other than Berlinghiero's son Barone, but the fact that all his known works are found in Florence makes it likely that he was Florentine. His heavily applied greenish-brown tones are cut through by streaks of light, by sudden and violent highlights that emphasize and agitate the facial features, giving them a strong and sometimes fiercely expressionistic cast. This leads us to believe that the Bardi Master is not the same person who painted the dossale (plate 28 and fig. 41) depicting *Saint Michael the Archangel, Enthroned* in the Church of Sant'Angelo at Vico l'Abate near Florence. The latter's accentuated graphic stylization of faces and drapery does resemble the Bardi Master but here is handled with a more subtle and planned sense of balance that also is reflected in the arrangement and composition of the scenes. The scenes are decked in clear, enamel-like colors; the jeweled tunics worn by the characters, the architecture, the landscape, the flowers — every detail takes on an aspect of exquisite unreality and a gorgeously decorative elegance.

The tendency to create a sort of plastic illusionism around the abstract graphic formulations of the Byzantine style is characteristic of all middle thirteenth-century Florentine painting. Its strongest and most representative manifestation is found in the work of Coppo di Marcovaldo. Documents tell us that he was in Florence in 1260; in September of that year he took part in the battle of Montaperti. Taken prisoner by the Sienese, he painted the *Bardonne Madonna* for the Church of the Servi (perhaps in exchange for his

31

freedom), which he signed and dated 1261. Just as in Guido da Siena's *Maestà*, the principal figures of this panel were gone over in the early Trecento by one of Duccio's followers. A large *Crucifix with Scenes from the Passion* (plate 26; figs. 37 and 38) in San Gimignano's Museo Civico probably belongs to the same period of Coppo's stay in Siena, while the typology of the faces in the Sienese *Madonna and Child*, perceptible now only by radiographic means, is reflected by the analogous composition (plate 27; figs. 39 and 40) that Coppo painted a few years later for the Servite Order at Orvieto. The strong plastic imprint of Coppo's painting is not the result of a rational construction, coldly devised to manipulate the Byzantine calligraphy, but rather of a profound emotional drive which the dramatic and sentimental strains within this calligraphy had infused with a fresh and powerful sense of solidity and unity. What does it matter that these schemata and formulas already had been discarded as outmoded, when they still serve so beautifully to express Coppo's burning participation in the sublime tragedy of Christ's agony (as in the San Gimignano *Crucifixion*) or the solemn majesty of his Madonnas in their gold-shot mantles? In this respect, Coppo finds his ideal predecessor in Giunta Pisano, although he surpasses Giunta in the heady orchestration of his emotions — in the San Gimignano scenes and, above all, in the shattering vision of hell in the dome of the Florentine Baptistry, which he clearly designed together with other sections of this outstanding mosaic group. Coppo's son Salerno might well have helped to design the cartoons for these mosaics. Salerno is documented at Pistoia in 1274 and 1276 and consequently credited with a *Crucifixion* in the Cathedral, done with his father. The Florentine painter Migliore also worked on the cartoons: he, like Coppo, had taken part in the battle of Montaperti and in 1271 signed and dated a panel (fig. 15), *The Redeemer Flanked by the Virgin and Saints Peter, John the Evangelist, and Paul*, now in the Uffizi. His dossale (fig. 17) of the *Madonna Flanked by Saints Peter and Paul and Four Scenes from Their Lives* in the Church of San Leolino at Panzano is probably earlier than the 1271 panel. Here, Migliore's work closely resembles that of the Master of Bigallo, but "with a calm and harmonious rhythmic accent that unites a strong decorative effect with a piquant byplay of affectionate details" (Ragghianti). This is not the place to contest Migliore's title to several paintings generally attributed to a Master of Bagano, so called after an elegant *Madonna* in a church in the village of Bagano. Their particular stylistic affinity to Coppo di Marcovaldo is witnessed further in the probable collaboration of the two masters on the formidable enterprise of the Baptistry mosaics, as well as on the breathtaking relief (fig. 18), *The Enthroned Madonna, Two Scenes, and Several Saints* in the Church of Santa Maria Maggiore in Florence.

According to one theory (Procacci's), the numerous paintings traditionally grouped under the single authorship of the Master of the Magdalen are actually the output of a company of painters. Indeed, it is difficult to trace a coherent line of development through the proliferation of variations on the cultural theme given by the individual paintings, which sometimes lead to pronounced qualitative differences. What brings them together is a certain "affinity with mosaics: broad and elementary structure, contrasting alternations of color, and hard, bristling outlines" (Marcucci). Such affinity is a characteristic aspect of a large part of Florentine painting during the last third of the thirteenth century; it is explained by the fact that Florence was the only place on the Italian mainland to produce a complex of mosaics bearing comparison with those of Venice or Sicily.

Fig. 18 - COPPO DI MARCOVALDO and MIGLIORE (attributed), *The Enthroned Madonna, Two Scenes, and Several Saints*, Church of Santa Maria Maggiore, Florence

Under the dome of Florence's Baptistry, Florentine painters up to Cimabue and Giotto designed the cartoons for these mosaics, working side by side with masters invited from Venice and, perhaps, from Greece and the Far East.

The Master of the Magdalen takes his name from what is perhaps his least felicitous work — a panel (plates 29 and 30; figs. 42 and 43) of *Saint Mary Magdalene with Eight Scenes from Her Life* in the Accademia Gallery in Florence. Although graphically crude, the colors are sparkling and the scenes are as fresh and direct as folk tales. Some of the other works are much finer; an altar frontal (fig. 24) in the Musée des Arts Décoratifs in Paris is a real masterpiece, with graceful characterizations and light, deft contours (compare, for example, with the gross, metallic contours of an analogous frontal in New York); the clear, lapidary colors of a *Saint Luke* in the Uffizi redeem its graphically mechanistic design.

Cenni di Pepo, known as Cimabue, is the conclusive figure in Florentine painting before the appearance of Giotto, and conclusive as well in the total development of the Italian Byzantine. From documents we learn only that he was a native of Florence and was in Rome in 1272 and Pisa in 1301 and 1302, where he did the figure of Saint John in the apse mosaic of the Cathedral. He died at Pisa around 1303. With some notable exceptions, modern criticism has now more or less accepted his title to a series of panels and frescoes, which, except for the documented Pisan *Saint John*, have a much-disputed chronology. They still provide us with a fairly consistent picture of what is without question the greatest inspiration in Duecento painting. The initial work of this series is generally agreed to be the large *Crucifix* (fig. 19) in Arezzo's Church of San Domenico. It is inspired by Giunta Pisano's Crucifixions but marked with a new and more trenchant precision of forms, perhaps inspired by Coppo di Marcovaldo, that also takes the direction of clear and vigorous composition. Christ's suffering body twists itself up to the very border of the Crucifix in a dreadful arch. His joints strain spasmodically; the features, muscles, and anatomical details, defined with rough energy in lines and chiaroscuro, take on almost trance-like perspectives. Yet, the overall composition unfolds in stately and harmonious rhythms, controlled and defined by strong outlines.

A second wonderful *Crucifix* (plate 33) in the Museo dell'Opera di Santa Croce in Florence is some years later than the Arezzo Crucifix. The overwrought Byzantine graphic style is still maintained in the pinched and saddened masklike faces of the Madonna and Saint John; however, it is much subdued in the subtlety pathetic, one might even say humanly felt, face of Christ, and dispensed with completely in the smooth conformations of the body. Among other things, the stylized tripartite division of the abdomen has disappeared. The transition from the Arezzo Crucifix to the Santa Croce Crucifix, a signal event in Cimabue's stylistic development, also is decisive in his evolution from Byzantine metaphor to a plastic type of reality. The sculptural concreteness of this new reality does not come from straining the limits of form and the preestablished figurative devices and symbols but springs from a new understanding of the body and its internal structure. Cimabue's stay in Rome, which exposed him not only to the classical world, but to the free, imaginative, and moving expressions of the late Roman period and the painting of the Paleo-Christian and Romanesque eras, probably contributed to his rediscovery of this new and, at the same time, venerable truth — the very same one that ten years earlier had broken through the superficiality of an overrefined classicism to blaze forth in the stirring

Fig. 19 - CIMABUE (CENNI DI PEPO), *Crucifix*, Church of San Domenico, Arezzo

Fig. 20 - CIMABUE (CENNI DI PEPO), *The Madonna of the Angels*, The Louvre, Paris

Romanesque figurations of Nicola Pisano's earliest pulpit.

While their specific problems of form were different, this eminent sculptor and Cimabue are brought together by the historically similar need to break free of a stultifying tradition. The parallel is strengthened by assigning Cimabue's large panel, now in The Louvre, *The Madonna of the Angels* (fig. 20) to this period, i.e., shortly after 1272. Toesca observed that this painting seems based on a study of ancient marbles, as if Cimabue now were looking beyond the classicism of the Byzantine tradition to the classicism of Nicola Pisano and his followers. Originally the painting was in the Church of San Francesco in Pisa. If we take this as evidence of an early sojourn by the artist at Pisa, we can also explain by this route the important and unmistakable connections between Cimabue and, for example, the Master of San Martino. In any event, this work, with its beautiful sense of sculptural relief, has a certain workmanlike inflexibility about the steady, symmetrical ascent of the angels along the sides of the throne and the pose of the Child, which happens to recall none other than the little Jesus in the Pisan altarpiece in the Church of San Martino. Difficult to justify in terms of some sort of outside assistance, this rigidity is logically explained in relation to the work that follows — *The Madonna and Child* (plates 31 and 32; figs. 44 and 45) — formerly in the Church of Santa Trinità in Florence and now in the Uffizi.

In this painting, the figure of the Virgin is raised high on an elaborate throne flanked by four pairs of angels, who carry the cadence of its steadily ascending lines into the background. The Virgin seems to float above the throne's arched dais like some majestic vision looming from the pinnacle of a resplendent apse. The work's unifying sense of perspective

36

helps to resolve the old Byzantine hierarchism into the architectonic and swelling monumentality of its austerely organic composition. But more than this, it is the incisive quality of the line that renders the panel so powerfully new and expressive. The broken and unchecked intensity of the outlines now gives a sense of three-dimensionality, of throbbing solidity, in contrast to the flat, silken surfaces, and now imparts an urgent dynamism to the figures. Typical are the three-quarter portraits of the four prophets. Squeezed into the cramped arches beneath the throne, they strain upward in sudden contortions that reflect a bursting inner tension. These prophets are blood brothers of the characters sculpted by Giovanni Pisano, that hang howling from the façade of the Cathedral in Florence.

Similar breeds of humanity populate Cimabue's frescoes for the choir and transept of the Basilica of San Francesco in Assisi, which probably were begun in 1277–80, during Nicholas III Orsini's pontificate. We cannot dwell upon this group of frescoes since it lies outside our present discussion of panel paintings, though they mark a turning point in the fortunes of Italian painting. It treats the most solemn and impassioned devotional themes and meditations of the Franciscan movement, including events in the life of the Virgin, the miracles performed by the Prince of Apostles, the Crucifixion, and the terrifying visions of the Apocalypse. These are interpreted with an imaginative drive revealed in the new layout of the composition, which boldly upsets the rhythmic spacing inherited from the strict liturgical tradition of Byzantium, and also in the moving characterizations and a three-dimensional unity of execution, still evident despite heavy deterioration. This truly terrifying work was followed by a delicate *Maestà with Saint Francis* in the Lower Church at Assisi, possibly by a large and hotly disputed *Enthroned Madonna and Two Angels* in the Church of Santa Maria dei Servi in Bologna, and by the mosaic *Saint John* at Pisa, which already possesses a sculptural simplicity and integrity worthy of Arnolfo. With the Assisi fresco group, Italian painting bids a solemn farewell to medieval Byzantinism. The *novus ordo* that will reign, not only through Giotto in Tuscany, but in the whole Latin world of art, is already in the wind.

We shall now turn our attention, briefly, to the other regions of Italy. The North and the South of Italy down to Sicily contain several regions abounding in outstanding groups of frescoes and mosaics that sometimes outshine in importance all of Tuscan painting before Cimabue. However, as far as panel painting is concerned, no region can match the rich, organic variety and the originality of Tuscany's output. Tuscany truly laid the groundwork for this art form and saw it flourish to such a degree that local traditions often gave way to its characteristic cultural forms, producing works that, more or less, are of a Tuscan stamp. Such is the case in Venice before the late but luxurious flowering of the Madonnieri workshops. Latium, including Southern Umbria, was perhaps the only region (in this case we actually should say area) in which panel painting sprang up and developed independently of Tuscany and, in addition, did not simply mirror the fresco and mosaic but created its own style and aesthetic values.

In Rome, the practice of painting on wood panels goes back to extremely ancient religious and iconographic traditions. Some very early examples of the genre, painted in encaustic on linen cloth attached to a piece of wood, have been identified, such as the fifth-century *Madonna* of Santa Maria Nova or the eighth-century *Madonna of Mercy* in Santa Maria in Trastevere. A more direct link with early traditions can be traced through the widespread diffusion, during the twelfth and thirteenth centuries, of a type known as the *Avvocata* (Our Lady who intercedes with God on behalf of Mankind), a half-figure of the Madonna unaccompanied by the Child. We know of at least a dozen copies and variants of this type, which, according to a revered tradition, is derived from a prototype icon painted by Saint Luke. The earliest of these is a heavily retouched version in the Church of Santa Maria in Aracoeli, attributed to the sixth century; the earliest of the Avvocatas painted during the twelfth and thirteenth centuries is the one in the Cathedral of Vetralla, attributed to the beginning of the twelfth century.

The recognized masterpiece of the Roman school is the triptych (plate 34) with hinged side panels of the *Redeemer Giving Blessing* flanked by the *Madonna Avvocata* and *Saint John the Evangelist* (who replaces the Baptist of the traditional *Deësis*) with scenes depicting the *Virgin's Dream* and the *Ascension of Saint John*. It too is derived from an image believed to be of miraculous origin — the Archeroptic (not fashioned by human hands) Christ, worshiped in the Sanctum Sanctorum. Ascribed to the sixth or seventh century, the original is all but buried under several successive repaintings. The triptych has been attributed to a period somewhere in the first half of the twelfth century and is one of the best and most aristocratic expressions of the Byzantine use of line. A highly stylized texture of minute folds through the Redeemer's refulgent mantle resembles the whorling grain of some fine wood. Despite this marked stylization, the lines of the drapery convey depths of relief in the same way that contour lines on a map show the various levels of the terrain — but not in the mechanical fashion this suggests. A range of heavy and fine lines are spaced across in subtle gradations; their elegant permutations reflect the same fine-honed and delicate sensitivity that gives gentleness to the Saviour's noble, severe face and lends a human sense of hidden foreboding to the faces of the Virgin and the Evangelist.

A diversity of styles marks the many versions of this venerated figure found in Latium, including one in the parish of Casape near Tivoli — deftly drawn but with all its drapery repainted — a number in the cathedrals of Tarquinia and Sutri and the Church of Santa Maria at Capranica and a version (plate 35) in Santa Maria Assunta at Trevignano. The laterals of this last are extant, and the painting is signed by the Roman painters Nicolò di Pietro Paolo and his son Pietro. These two masters probably were active during the first decades of the thirteenth century. They also are credited with a panel of the *Enthroned Madonna and Child* in the Sanctuary of the Madonna del Sorbo at Campagnano in the Viterbo region.

We do not know whether the Niccolò who signed the Trevignano triptych is the same Niccolò whose name — together with the name Giovanni — appears on a panel (plate 36) in the Vatican Pinacoteca. The panel is curious and unique in shape; it is a large tondo with a predella-shaped extension at the bottom. A vertical series of five scenes portray the *Last Judgment* and the *Works of Corporal Mercy*. There is a recurring hypothesis that the Niccolò and Giovanni of the Vatican tondo were two of the several painters of the famous frescoes in the church at Castello Sant'Elia, near Nepi. They depict the *Transfiguration*, the *Madonna*, the *Twenty-Four Elders of the Apocalypse*, the *Female Saints Handing*

Out Crowns, and various other apocalyptic scenes and bear the Latin inscription: "Johannes and Stephanus, brother Roman painters, and Nicolaus, Johannes' real nephew." Lack of secure reference points makes the chronological order of all these paintings extremely difficult to ascertain and open to wide margins of error, as is the case with the Roman school in general. The Nepi frescoes probably are somewhat older than the others; anyway, this is a largely homogeneous movement, in which early traces of classicism gradually yielded to Byzantine influence, which began to make a marked appearance during the first decades of the thirteenth century. The gates then were opened to Tuscan elements (the Madonnas of San Cosmo e Damiano and Santa Maria al Foro Traiano; the Crucifix in the Collegio Angelico); lastly, around the turn of the fourteenth century, the movement comes under the powerful sway of Pietro Cavallini.

Fig. 21 - ALBERTO DI SOZIO, *Crucifix,* Duomo, Spoleto

The painting of Southern Umbria had initial connections with Roman activity, primarily through their common derivation from the miniaturistic style of Benedictine manuscripts radiating from the Abbey of Monte Cassino. The important center of Southern Umbrian painting was Spoleto. During the last half of the twelfth century, there worked at Spoleto a certain Alberto di Sozio; his name and the date 1187 are written on a *Crucifix* (fig. 21) in the Cathedral. It comes from the Church of San Giovanni e Paolo, where Alberto has painted some beautiful frescoes. The painting may not be the earliest Crucifixion in Southern Umbria, but it is a perfect example of the region's culture, which still was essentially Romanesque; the Christ is shown alive, and a temperate use of line fits in with vigorous efforts at plastic form. This culture, which also shows mild Byzantine leanings, occurs both locally and in its early Duecento diffusion toward Latium (the triptych in Santa Maria Nova at Viterbo), the Marches, and the Abruzzi, reaching as far as the area of Siena (we have pointed out that Siena's earliest painting is tied in with that of Spoleto). We know the names of Spoletine painters who on occasion worked away from their native city; through them the tradition followed by Alberto di Sozio came into contact with more recent developments. A certain Petrus signed and dated 1241 (or 1242) a *Cruci-fixion* in the Church of San Antonio in Campi di Norcia, which reflects early stirrings of Giunta's influence. There is a Rinaldo (or Rinaldictus) di Ranuccio, who signed two Cruci-fixes strongly redolent of Giunta; one is in the Fabriano Pinacoteca and the other, dated 1265, in the Bologna Pinacoteca. Simeone and Machilone produced a Crucifix dated 1258 coming from the Cathedral of San Silvestro in Ancona (it was formerly in Professor R. Bastianelli's private collection in Rome and is now in the Palazzo Venezia) and a handsome dossale of the *Enthroned Madonna and Four Scenes from Her Life* in the Mayer Van den Bergh Museum at Antwerp; the latter, however, already has been drawn into the Flor-entine orbit revolving around the Master of Bigallo and Coppo di Marcovaldo.

Northern Umbrian panel painting presents a different stylistic picture. Assisi was its main center of activity. An occasional rare thirteenth-century Crucifixion was uninfluenced by Giunta Pisano, such as the one now in the Church of Santa Chiara that is famous for having spoken to Saint Francis in San Dominiano; vigorous plastic form and warm colors liken it to early Luccan Crucifixes. Another, in the treasury of the Basilica of San Fran-cesco, clearly derives from Spoleto. With such exceptions, Northern Umbria is the scene of Giunta Pisano's most widespread and organic influence. As we have mentioned, Giunta painted two Crucifixions at Assisi; one, with signature, is in Santa Maria degli Angioli and the other, now lost, is known to have borne the date 1236. Giunta's major disciple, the so-called Master of Saint Francis — he takes his name from a *Saint Francis Flanked by Two Angels* (plate 37) painted on the wooden pallet on which the Saint died and located in Santa Maria degli Angioli in Assisi — is the dominant figure in all North Umbrian painting of the latter Duecento. Curiously, works inspired by Giunta only begin to appear in Umbria a good twenty years after his supposed stay there. Edward B. Garrison attempts to ex-plain this circumstance, at least in part, by Frederick II's fight with the Church. The only dated painting by the Master of Saint Francis is in fact from 1272. This is a large *Crucifix* (plate 38) from the Church of San Francesco at Prato, now in the Galleria Nazionale dell'Umbria at Perugia. Here, the harsh dramatic tension of Giunta's treatment has changed to a gentler one through flowing linear rhythms that impart a stately decorative effect to the deeply curved body of the Christ. Giunta's bronze-like skin tones have been replaced by softly shaded tones of light and delicate hue. Among other things, the figures of the sorrowing Madonna and Saint John in the capricroce are full length, replacing the usual busts, and a tiny figure of Saint Francis kneels at Christ's feet. Despite a grandiose layout, the Perugia Crucifix is a work of highly refined elegance and is not lacking in graphic facil-ity. The painting of Saint Francis follows this tendency to the verge of the grotesque. The Saint's miniscule face perches over the exaggerated length of his body; the once stiff cassock is loosely draped in supple folds. The body's curvature is carried to an extreme in a *Crucifixion* in the Stoclet collection in Brussels, ascribed by some critics — together with a *Crucifixion* in the Acton collection in Florence — to the Master of Saint Francis. The attributions seem correct and lead us to conclude that the painter's ever-sharpening linear sensitivity was burning its way toward full and resonant emphasis on the figure, one of the strongest this century had witnessed, judging from the supercharged group of mourners in the tabellone of the Brussels Crucifix. Several side panels with the figures of saints in Brussels, New York, Perugia, and Washington probably are parts of a dossale

40

Fig. 22 - MASTER OF SAINT FRANCIS, *The Descent from the Cross*, Galleria Nazionale dell'Umbria, Perugia

Fig. 23 - MASTER OF SAINT FRANCIS, *The Pietà*, Galleria Nazionale dell'Umbria, Perugia

from which the middle section is missing. Two scenes (figs. 22 and 23) depicting the *Descent from the Cross* and *The Pietà* in the Galleria in Perugia also are part of a dossale painted by the Master of Saint Francis. These are analogous to several fresco *Scenes from the Passion* in the Lower Church of San Francesco at Assisi; together with several *Scenes from the Life of Saint Francis* in the same church, they show the fundamental importance in Umbrian painting of the Master's fresco work as well.

There is a large body of Umbrian works that reflect the Master of Saint Francis' linear interpretation of Giunta's style, suggesting that he had a large following. Some of these painters rise above the rank of follower; though weaned on the Master's style, they developed their own independent directions. First to appear was the Master of Saint Clare, named after a panel (plate 39) dated 1238 in the Church of Santa Chiara in Assisi, which portrays *Saint Clare with Eight Scenes from Her Life*. The same church contains a *Crucifixion* that the Master painted for Donna Benedetta, who followed Saint Clare as Abbess. Since Benedetta died in 1260 and the Crucifix is styled on the one painted by the Master of San Martino in 1272, we assume that the work was executed several years after the death of its patroness. He also is credited with a panel, *Enthroned Madonna and Child*, also in Santa Chiara. The scenes from the life of Saint Clare give us the full measure of this anonymous Master's seething inspiration. The first ever created for the Saint, his iconographic motifs reveal an expressive immediacy, a wealth of fresh imagery and situations that have not a trace of Byzantine cant. Thus, he returns to the unfettered traditions of the Western Romanesque style, bringing them into step with a historical era that in Umbria already was witnessing the splendors of Cimabue's dawn.

The Master of Farneto had contacts not only with Cimabue but with Giotto's work in Assisi, during his earliest period of activity before the celebrated Franciscan cycle. The style of the Master of Farneto recently has been analyzed by Roberto Longhi on the basis of a dossale in the Perugia Gallery from the Franciscan Convent of Farneto.

The last twenty years of the Duecento in Umbria blaze with activity, thanks to the Tuscan and Roman masters that had gathered to decorate Assisi's Basilica of San Francesco. The last outstanding Umbrian figure of the century is the Cesi Master. His activity continued into the first decade of the fourteenth century, as shown by the date 1308 on the work from which he takes his name, a beautiful *Enthroned Madonna Surrounded by Two Angels and Eight Apostles* located in the tiny Cesi Museum near Terni.

Emilia is another region where Giunta's influence was important, particularly at Bologna, where there are several Crucifixes (one in the Pinacoteca Pubblica, two in the Church of San Francesco, and one in the Church of Santa Maria in Borgo) that formerly were attributed as related to the work of the Master of Saint Francis. They doubtlessly owe their derivation to the Pisan artist's stay at Bologna, recorded by the well-known Crucifix in San Domenico, whereas Cimabue's *Madonna* in the Church of Santa Maria dei Servi created hardly a stir. The region produced some eminent frescoes (for example, the decoration of the dome of the Baptistry of Parma) but is singularly poor in panel paintings. In the other trans-Apennine regions, panel paintings either are scarce or strictly mediocre.

The one exception is a panel (plates 40 and 41; figs. 46–48), painted on both sides, of the *Madonna and Child* and *Scenes from the Life of Saint Agatha* in the Church of Sant'Agata in Cremona. Possibly this work can be dated as early as the last decade of the Duecento. As Salmi noted, its artist probably was a miniaturist trained in the Paduan-Venetian Byzantine style but responsive to the influence of Cimabue. His distinguishing characteristic is an unconstrained and fervid expressiveness, pungent with realistic temperamental attitudes. This quality has earned the painting an overenthusiastic re-evaluation in some critical circles, although, not infrequently, it treads a fine line between folk-art freshness and a decidedly low and intimate boldness. Exceptional colors are laid on briskly with a flowing hand and skillful highlights, attesting the painting's cultural origins. But the swaddled figures in their heavy, swollen drapery writhe in a violent pantomine of gestures that reduces any dramatic effectiveness to confusion, caricature, or downright vulgarity such as we find in the gathered Apostles (a sort of Pentecost without the Virgin), or Saint Agatha spurning the enticements offered by the old hag Aphrodesia, or even in the Young Jesus who proceeds Saint Peter on a visit to the prison ("a meddling little street urchin, all eyes and ears and inborn spunk," as he has been described).

The Master of Saint Agatha is without question a powerful and original artist, but his glory also is his limitation; because of the unresolved conflict between the refined maturity of his palette and technique and the raw edges of a nature geared to prosaic and realistic description, he was fated to be unique. And so he was; he had neither precedent nor following in the century that had learned to restore a stirring human significance and transfiguring lyric quality to the aristocratic formulas and conventions of the ancient tradition of Byzantium.

42

Fig. 24 - MASTER OF THE MAGDALEN (attributed), *Madonna and Child, Flanked by Saints Andrew and James and Six Scenes,* Musée des Arts Décoratifs, Paris

SELECTED BIBLIOGRAPHY

BOLOGNA, F. *La pittura italiana delle Origini,* Dresden and Rome, 1962

CARLI, E. *La pittura medievale pisana,* Milan, 1958

———. *La pittura senese,* Milan, 1955

COLETTI, L. *I primitivi: dai Benedettini a Giotto,* Novara, 1941

GARRISON, E. B. *Italian Romanesque Panel Painting,* Florence, 1949

LONGHI, R. "Giudizio sul Duecento," *Proporzioni,* II (1948)

MARCUCCI, L. *Le Gallerie Nazionali di Firenze: I dipinti toscani del XIII secolo,* Rome, 1958

RAGGHIANTI, C. L. *La pittura del Duecento a Firenze,* Florence, 1955

SALVINI, R. *Cimabue,* Rome, 1946

SANDBERG VALVALÀ, E. *La Croce dipinta italiana,* Verona, 1929

SINIBALDI, G., and BRUNETTI, G. *Pittura italiana del Duecento e Trecento* (catalogue of the Giotto Exhibition), Florence, 1943

TOESCA, P. *Storia dell'arte italiana,* Vol. I: *Il Medioevo,* Turin, 1927

VAN MARLE, R. *Le scuole della pittura italiana,* Vol. I, The Hague and Milan, 1932

COLORPLATES

Plate 2

MASTER OF THE OBLATE CRUCIFIX

(Luccan, mid-13th century)

Crucifixion with Four Scenes from the Passion

This panel is part of a diptych from the Convent of Santa Chiara in Lucca. It is attributed to a follower of Bonaventura Berlinghieri who derives his name from a Crucifixion in the Oblate Convent at Florence. *Mary Fainting* and *Mary Receiving Saint John as Her Son* are portrayed at the sides of the Corpus. At the bottom are shown *The Ascent to Calvary* and *The Descent from the Cross*. The companion panel (fig. 6) contains *The Madonna and Child* surrounded by Saints Peter, John the Baptist, Clare, Andrew, Anthony, Francis, the Archangel Michael, and Jacob.

40$^1/_2$ x 24″. Galleria dell'Accademia, Florence

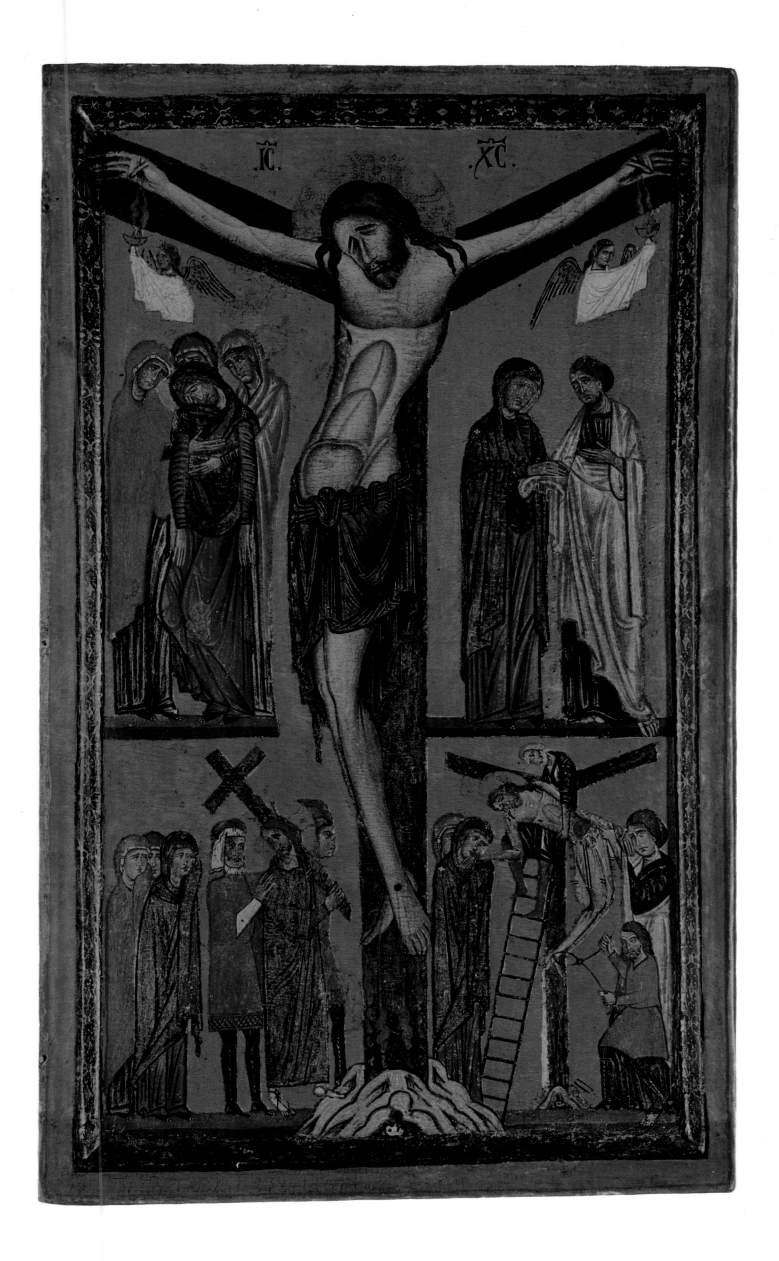

Fig. 25 - MASTER OF THE OBLATE CRUCIFIX, *The Ascent to Calvary* (detail of plate 2)

Plate 3

MASTER OF THE OBLATE CRUCIFIX

The Descent from the Cross (detail of plate 2)

Plate 4

MASTER OF THE ACCADEMIA CRUCIFIX

(Pisan, end of the 12th century)

Crucifix with Scenes from the Passion

Of unknown origin, this painting was moved from the Accademia to the Uffizi in recent years. The left part of the tabellone shows *Christ Washing the Feet of the Disciples, The Betrayal,* and *The Flagellation.* The right part shows *The Descent from the Cross, The Entombment,* and *The Descent into Hell.* The left capricroce contains *The Virgin and Saint John* and the right (partly destroyed) a *Holy Woman.*

12′4³/₈″ x 91″. Uffizi Gallery, Florence

Plate 5

MASTER OF THE ACCADEMIA CRUCIFIX

The Betrayal (detail of plate 4)

Plate 6

Master of the San Sepolcro Crucifix

(Pisan, end of the 12th century)

Crucifix with Scenes from the Passion

This originally came from the Church of San Sepolcro in Pisa, and is sometimes designated "Crucifix No. 15" after its number in the Museum's Catalogue. The finial of the Cross shows *The Ascension*, the left capricroce *The Last Supper*, while the right contains *Christ Washing the Feet of the Disciples*. Reading from left to right, the tabellone shows: *The Mocking of Christ, Jesus Being Offered the Vinegar-Soaked Sponge, The Three Marys at the Sepulchre, The Road to Emmaus* and *The Supper at Emmaus, Christ Appearing at the Supper,* and *Christ Appearing at the Closed Gates.* The panel at the foot of the Cross contains a *Pentecost.*

111 x 93³/₄". Museo Nazionale di San Matteo, Pisa

Plate 7

MASTER OF THE SAN SEPOLCRO CRUCIFIX

The Mocking of Christ and *The Three Marys at the Sepulchre* (detail of plate 6)

Figs. 26 & 27 - MASTER OF THE SAN MATTEO CRUCIFIX, *Four Scenes from the Passion* (detail of plate 8)

Plate 8

MASTER OF THE SAN MATTEO CRUCIFIX

(Pisan, beginning of the 13th century)

Crucifix with Scenes from the Passion

Originally in the Monastery of San Matteo at Pisa, this work is usually designated as "Crucifix No. 20" after its number in the Museum's Catalogue. It is painted on parchment which was then attached to wood. The finial shows *The Ascension*, and *The Virgin and Saint John* and *The Two Marys* are depicted on the capricroce. The left side of the tabellone contains *The Descent from the Cross, The Pietà*, and *The Entombment*. The right side displays *The Three Marys at the Sepulchre, The Road to Emmaus* and *The Supper at Emmaus*, and *The Incredulity of Thomas. The Descent into Hell* is shown on the bottom panel.

117³/₈ x 91³/₄". Museo Nazionale di San Matteo, Pisa

Fig. 28 - FOLLOWER OF GIUNTA PISANO, *Processional Cross* (detail of plate 9)

Plate 9

FOLLOWER OF GIUNTA PISANO

(Pisan, first half of the 13th century)

Processional Cross

Painted on both sides, this Crucifix comes from the Vallombrosa Monastery near San Paolo at Ripa d'Arno, Pisa.

44½ x 32⅝″. Museo Nazionale di San Matteo, Pisa

Fig. 29 - PISAN MASTER, *The Beheading of Saint Catherine* (detail of plate 10)

Plate 10

PISAN MASTER

(Pisan, last half of the 13th century)

Saint Catherine of Alexandria with Eight Scenes from Her Life

This panel came from the Church of San Silvestro at Pisa. To the left of the central figure are *Saint Catherine Professing the Faith, Saint Catherine Disputing with the Philosophers, Angels Visiting Saint Catherine in Prison,* and *The Condemnation of Saint Catherine.* To the right are *The Martyrdom of Saint Catherine, The Beheading of Saint Catherine, The Burial of Saint Catherine,* and *Angels Bearing Saint Catherine to Heaven.*

44 $^{1}/_{2}$ x 42 $^{1}/_{8}$". Museo Nazionale di San Matteo, Pisa

SCA CATERINA OCC... ...LATVR...

SCA ... ...GE...LITVRA ...DE LIBVS...

Fig. 30 - PISAN MASTER, *The Burial of Saint Catherine* (detail of plate 10)

Plate 11

PISAN MASTER

Saint Catherine Disputing with the Philosophers and *Angels Visiting Saint Catherine in Prison* (detail of plate 10)

Plate 12

The Annunciation to Saint Anne, Saint Anne and a Serving-Woman, and *Angels Assisting Saint Joachim at His Sacrifice.* These are details from the altarpiece, *Enthroned Madonna and Child and Ten Scenes from the Legend of Anne and Joachim,* also known as the *Madonna of San Martino,* since it originally came from the Church of San Martino at Pisa (the entire work is shown in fig. 12).

63 x 43¹/₈″ (entire altarpiece). Museo Nazionale di San Matteo, Pisa

Plate 13

Saint Joachim Heading Home with His Flock (detail of fig. 12)

Plate 14

MASTER OF SAN MARTINO

The Birth of the Virgin (detail of fig. 12)

Fig. 31 - MASTER OF SAN MARTINO, *The Young Madonna* (detail of plate 15)

Plate 15

MASTER OF SAN MARTINO

Saint Anne, Enthroned, Holding the Young Madonna

Possibly from the Monastery of Sant'Anna at Pisa.

49⅝ x 29⅞″. Museo Nazionale di San Matteo, Pisa

Plate 16

Margaritone d'Arezzo

(Aretine, last half of the 13th century)

Saint Francis of Assisi

A painting of unknown origin, signed at the bottom: *"Margaritus de Arito me F."* ("Margarito of Arezzo painted this work").

39³/₅ x 15³/₄". Pinacoteca Nazionale, Siena

Plate 17

GUIDO DA SIENA

(Sienese, last half of the 13th century)

Madonna and Child

This work comes from the Church of the Confraternità di Santa Maria degli Angioli (later known as the Church of San Bernardino). It was cut down to its present dimensions during the eighteenth century. Old documents reveal that at the bottom of the complete panel there was an inscription: "ISTA TABULA EST FRATERNITATIS BEATE MARIAE SEMPER VIRGINIS QUAM FECIT FIERI IN A.D. MCCLXVII" ("This panel belongs to the brotherhood of Blessed Mary, Ever Virgin, and was painted in the Year of Our Lord 1267").

55 $^1/_8$ x 38 $^1/_4$". Pinacoteca Nazionale, Siena

Fig. 32 - FOLLOWER OF GUIDO DA SIENA, *The Nativity* (detail of plate 18)

Plate 18

FOLLOWER OF GUIDO DA SIENA

(Sienese, last half of the 13th century)

Saint Peter, Enthroned, Flanked by Six Scenes from the Gospels and the Life of Saint Peter

This comes from the now-destroyed Church of San Pietro in Bianchi at Siena. Reading from left to right, the episodes depicted are: *The Annunciation, The Nativity, The Calling of Peter and Andrew, An Angel Delivering Saint Peter from Prison, The Fall of Simon Magus,* and *The Martyrdom of Saint Peter.*

34¹/₄ x 65″. Pinacoteca Nazionale, Siena

Fig. 33 - FOLLOWER OF GUIDO DA SIENA, *An Angel Delivering Saint Peter from Prison* (detail of plate 18)

Plate 19

FOLLOWER OF GUIDO DA SIENA

The Annunciation (detail of plate 18)

Fig. 34 - SIENESE MASTER, *Saint John and Two Disciples Meeting Jesus; The Baptism of Christ; The Beheading of the Baptist; The Feast of Herod* (detail of plate 20)

Plate 20

SIENESE MASTER

(Sienese, last half of the 13th century)

Saint John the Baptist and Twelve Scenes from His Life

This comes from the Convent of Santa Petronilla at Siena. The left portion contains: *The Annunciation to Zacharias, The Visitation, The Birth of the Baptist, Saint Elizabeth Presenting the Infant Baptist to the Virgin and Child, An Angel Leading Saint John in the Wilderness.* The section on the right contains: *Saint John and Two Disciples Meeting Jesus, The Baptism of Christ, The Beheading of the Baptist, The Feast of Herod, Saint John in Limbo, Christ and the Virgin Receiving Saint John into Heaven.*

34¹/₄ x 65". Pinacoteca Nazionale, Siena

Plate 21

SIENESE MASTER

The Annunciation to Zacharias, The Visitation, The Birth of the Baptist, Saint Elizabeth Presenting the Infant Baptist to the Virgin and Child (detail of plate 20)

Plate 22

Master of the Blessed Gallerani

(Sienese, last half of the 13th century)

Saint Clare Fends Off a Saracen Attack on Her Convent by Displaying the Pyx

A detail from a diptych of unknown origin (possibly from the Basilica of San Domenico) depicting four episodes from the lives of Saints Francis, Clare, Bartholomew, and Catherine of Alexandria. The artist's name is drawn from another diptych in the same museum depicting scenes from the life of the Blessed Andrea Gallerani.

48 x 28″ (entire panel). Pinacoteca Nazionale, Siena

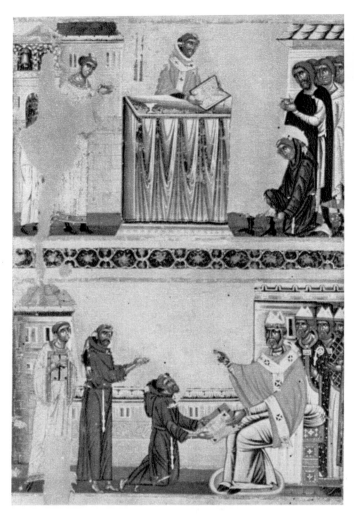

Figs. 35 & 36 - Master of the Bardi Saint Francis, *Saint Francis Removing His Sandals at the Porziuncola; The Pope Approving Saint Francis' Rule; Saint Francis at Communion; Saint Francis Exorcising a Demon from a Man Possessed* (detail of plate 24)

Plate 24

Master of the Bardi Saint Francis

(Florentine, mid-13th century)

Saint Francis of Assisi with Twenty Scenes from His Life

Beginning with the left-hand column, starting at the top, the scenes are as follows: *Saint Francis, Imprisoned by His Father, Is Freed by His Mother; Saint Francis Renounces His Worldly Possessions; Saint Francis Inscribing the Sign of the Cross on His Cassock; Saint Francis Removing His Sandals at the Porziuncola; The Pope Approving Saint Francis' Rule; Creating the First Representation of the Manger at Greccio; Saint Francis Preaching to the Birds; Saint Francis Preaching to the Sultan; Saint Francis Being Given the Sheep That Was Found Among the Goats; Saint Francis Saving Two Sheep by Exchanging Them for His Cloak; Saint Francis Receiving the Stigmata; Saint Francis Committing Himself to the Pillory for Having Eaten Meat; Saint Francis Appearing Before the Cathedral Chapter at Arles; Saint Francis Curing the Lepers; The Death of Saint Francis; Saint Francis Exorcising a Demon from a Man Possessed; Saint Francis at Communion; Saint Francis Saves a Boat from Shipwreck; Saint Francis Receiving Thanks for Performing a Miracle; Saint Francis Administering a Healing Bath to a Sick Man.*

92¹/₈ x 50″. Bardi Chapel, Church of Santa Croce, Florence

Plate 25

Saint Francis Preaching to the Birds and *Saint Francis Preaching to the Sultan* (detail of plate 24)

Figs. 37 & 38 - Coppo di Marcovaldo, *Four Scenes from the Passion* (detail of plate 26)

Plate 26

Coppo di Marcovaldo

(Florentine, last half of the 13th century)

Crucifix with Scenes from the Passion (detail)

Of unknown origin. The scenes depicted on the tabellone are: *The Betrayal of Christ, Christ Before Caiaphas, The Flagellation, The Mocking of Christ, The Crucifixion,* and *The Pietà.*

115³/₈ x 97¹/₄" (entire Crucifix). Museo Civico, San Gimignano

Figs. 39 & 40 - Coppo di Marcovaldo, *Angels* (detail of plate 27)

Plate 27

Coppo di Marcovaldo

Madonna and Child

The church in which this painting is now located is probably its original home.

93³/₄ x 53¹/₈″. Church of San Martino ai Servi, Orvieto

Fig. 41 - MASTER OF VICO L'ABATE, *The Archangel Michael Appearing to Christ* (detail from *Saint Michael the Archangel, Enthroned*)

Plate 28

MASTER OF VICO L'ABATE

(Florentine, mid-13th century)

The Bull Appearing on Mount Gargano

This is one of six scenes, three on each side, that flank the main figure in *Saint Michael the Archangel, Enthroned,* an altar frontal still in its original location.

38⁵/₈ x 48⁷/₈″ (entire panel). Church of Sant'Angelo, Vico l'Abate (Florence)

Figs. 42 & 43 - MASTER OF THE MAGDALEN, *The Communion of the Magdalen* and *The Burial of the Magdalen* (detail of plate 29)

Plate 29

MASTER OF THE MAGDALEN

(Florentine, mid-13th century)

Saint Mary Magdalene with Eight Scenes from Her Life and the Gospels

This panel was originally in a Florentine convent. Starting from the top and reading from left to right are the following scenes: *Mary Magdalene Annointing the Feet of Jesus; The Raising of Lazarus; Noli Me Tangere; Mary Magdalene Instructing the Disciples; The Ascension of the Magdalen; An Angel Bringing Bread to the Magdalen in the Wilderness; The Communion of the Magdalen; The Burial of the Magdalen.*

65 x 29⁷/₈″. Galleria dell'Accademia, Florence

NE DESP
ETIS.
UOSQUI
PECCARE
SOLETIS.
EXEMPLO
Q3 MEO.
UOS REPA
RATE DE
O :·

Plate 30

MASTER OF THE MAGDALEN

Noli Me Tangere (detail of plate 29)

Figs. 44 & 45 - CIMABUE (CENNI DI PEPO), *Angels* (detail of plate 31)

Plate 31

CIMABUE (CENNI DI PEPO)

(Florentine, last half of the 13th century)

Madonna and Child, Enthroned, with Eight Angels and Four Prophets

This comes from the Church of Santa Trinita at Florence, for which it was painted.

11′ 6¹/₂″ x 87³/₄″. Uffizi Gallery, Florence

Plate 32

CIMABUE (CENNI DI PEPO)

Madonna and Child (detail of plate 31)

Plate 33

CIMABUE (CENNI DI PEPO)

Crucifix

This Crucifix was executed for the Church of Santa Croce at Florence.

14′ 8³/₈″ x 12′ 9¹/₂″. Museo dell'Opera di Santa Croce, Florence

Plate 34

ROMAN MASTER

(Roman, first half of the 12th century)

The Redeemer Giving His Blessing, flanked by the *Madonna Avvocata* and *Saint John the Evangelist*

This triptych with extra panels has remained in its original location. Beneath the Madonna is a panel (not shown) depicting the *Dream of the Virgin*, and beneath Saint John is another, depicting the *Ascension of Saint John*.

58¹/₂ x 27⁵/₈″ (main panel). Duomo, Tivoli

Plate 35

Niccolò di Pietro Paolo and Pietro di Niccolò

(Romans, first half of the 13th century)

The Redeemer Giving His Blessing, flanked by the *Madonna Avvocata* and *Saint John the Evangelist*

The church in which this triptych hangs is probably its original location. On the exterior faces of the side wings are depicted Saints Peter and Paul. The inscription beneath Christ's throne reads: "nicolaus de petro paulo cu[m] filio suo petro picto[res] romani — ego archip[res]b[ite]r martin[us] pingere feci" ("Niccolò di Pietro Paolo and his son Peter, Roman painters –– I, Archbishop Martin ordered this picture to be made").

56³/₄ x 24³/₈". Church of Santa Maria Assunta, Trevignano

REX EGO SUM
CELI QVIDE PPLM
QVIDE MORE
REDE MI

Plate 36

Niccolò and Giovanni

(Roman, mid-13th century)

The Last Judgment and *The Works of Corporal Mercy*

This unusually shaped panel comes from the Convent of Santa Maria in Campo Marzio at Rome. Among other inscriptions, it bears the names of the painters, "NICOLAUS IOHANNES PICTOR[ES]."

113³/₄ x 95¹/₄". Pinacoteca Vaticana, Rome

Plate 37

Saint Francis Flanked by Two Angels

The panel employed in this painting was the wooden plank which served as Saint Francis' deathbed. This is attested by the inscription in the book which the Saint holds: "HIC MIHI VIVENTI LECTUS FUIT ET MORIENTI" ("This was my bed both in life and death"). The inscription on the lower half of the panel refers to Francis' stigmata. The unknown artist takes his name from this work.

42¹/₂ x 23¹/₄". Church of Santa Maria degli Angioli, Assisi

Plate 39

MASTER OF SAINT CLARE

(Umbrian, last half of the 13th century)

The Meeting of Saint Clare and Saint Francis

This detail is one of eight scenes flanking a portrait of Saint Clare. At the base of the entire panel is the inscription: "FACTE FUERUNT ISTE SUB ANNO D[OMI]NI INDIC. XI TEMPORE D[OMI]NI MARTINI PAPAE QUARTI" ("Made during the Year of Our Lord, 1283, the eleventh year of the pontificate of Pope Martin X").

110⁵/ₛ x 65³/ₛ" (entire panel). Church of Santa Chiara, Assisi

Fig. 46 - Master of Saint Agatha, *Pentecost* (detail of plate 40)

Plate 40

Master of Saint Agatha

(Paduan (?), second half of the 13th century)

Madonna and Child and *Pentecost*

Still in its original location, this panel is painted on both sides. The obverse contains *Scenes from the Life of Saint Agatha* (see plate 41). The Pentecost scene here shown refers to the Divine Grace that inspired Agatha's reply to her accuser, Quintianus, governor of Sicily.

44¹/₈ x 25⁵/₈″. Church of Sant'Agata, Cremona

Figs. 47 & 48 - Master of Saint Agatha, *Saint Agatha Refusing the Worldly Temptations Proffered by Aphrodesia* and *The Scourging of the Saint* (detail of plate 41)

Plate 41

Master of Saint Agatha

Scenes from the Life of Saint Agatha

The obverse of the panel shown in plate 40. The main scene is *Saint Paul, Preceded by the Child Jesus, Visiting Saint Agatha in Prison.* Along the top of the panel are the following: *Saint Agatha Refusing the Worldly Temptations Proffered by Aphrodesia; Saint Agatha Spurning the Suit of Quintianus; The Scourging of the Saint* and *Agatha Praying in Prison; The Martyrdom of Saint Agatha.* The bottom of the panel, partially shown, contains *Saint Agatha Thrown onto Burning Coals; The Earthquake; The Burial of Saint Agatha;* and *The Death of Quintianus.*